W9-BKA-282

Things That Go!

James Buckley, Jr.

SCHOLASTIC INC.

New York Toronto London Auckland
Sydney Mexico City New Delhi Hong Kong

EDUCATIONAL BOARD: Monique Datta, EdD, Asst. Professor, Rossier School of Education, USC; Karyn Saxon, PhD, Elementary Curriculum Coordinator, Wayland, MA; Francie Alexander, Chief Academic Officer, Scholastic Inc.

Copyright © 2013 by Scholastic Inc.

All rights reserved. Published by Scholastic Inc., *Publishers since 1920.*
SCHOLASTIC, SCHOLASTIC DISCOVER MORE™, and associated logos are trademarks and/or registered trademarks of Scholastic Inc.

No part of this publication may be reproduced,
stored in a retrieval system, or transmitted in any form
or by any means, electronic, mechanical, photocopying,
recording, or otherwise, without written permission of the publisher.
For information regarding permission, write to Scholastic Inc.,
Attention: Permissions Department, 557 Broadway, New York, NY 10012.

ISBN (Trade) 978-0-545-53376-8
ISBN (Clubs) 978-0-545-62399-5

12 11 10 9 8 7 6 5 4 3 2 1   13 14 15 16 17 18/0

Printed in the U.S.A.   40
This edition first printing, August 2013

Scholastic is constantly working to lessen the environmental
impact of our manufacturing processes. To view our
industry-leading paper procurement policy,
visit www.scholastic.com/paperpolicy.

Read more! Do more!

Download your free all-new digital book,
Things That Go! Reading Fun

Quizzes to test
your knowledge
and reading skills

Fun activities to
share what you've
discovered

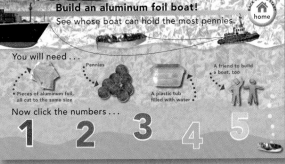

Log on to
www.scholastic.com/discovermore/readers
Enter this special code: L1DMC6HCG2P1

3

Stand up.

Go across
the room.

How did you
get there?

You
walked!

4

People also use machines to move around.

Cars, airplanes, boats, and more—here are many things that go!

The first bicycles
were hard to ride.
Riders sat up high.
They often fell off!

Be safe!
Wear a helmet

every time you
ride a bike.

Helmet

Handlebar

Brake

Pedal

Today, racers can ride safely at 50 miles per hour.

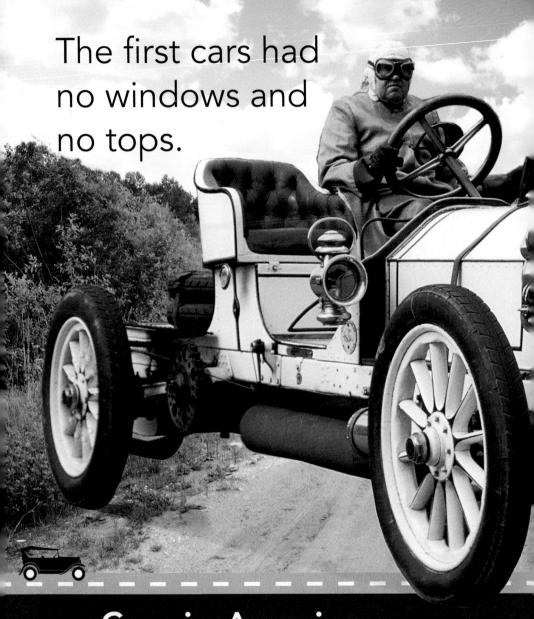

The first cars had no windows and no tops.

Cars in America

1912   1930   1956

The roads were dusty. Drivers wore gloves and goggles to stay clean.

NEW WORD

goggles

GAH-guhlz

Drivers wore **goggles** to keep dust and bugs out of their eyes.

SAY IT OUT LOUD

CR-468

1970   1992   2013

Car races test drivers and the cars that they drive.

Watch out for the corners. Don't slide!

Types of race cars

stock

Indy

drag

rally

In the past, strong horses pulled loaded wagons.

Then engines were invented. Trucks drove down new roads.

Now trucks haul big loads. They carry everything we need.

NEW WORD

haul

hawl

The bigger a truck is, the more it can **haul**.

SAY IT OUT LOUD

One engine plus
two wheels equals
a motorcycle.

Engin

Foot pedal

The rider twists
a hand grip.
Power goes to
the engine.

BUBBA STEWART

Hand grip

Bubba Stewart
won his first racing
championship when he
was six years old! Since
then, he has become one
of the best motocross
riders ever.

YOU CAN DO IT!

The rider uses
foot pedals
to change
gears and
to stop.

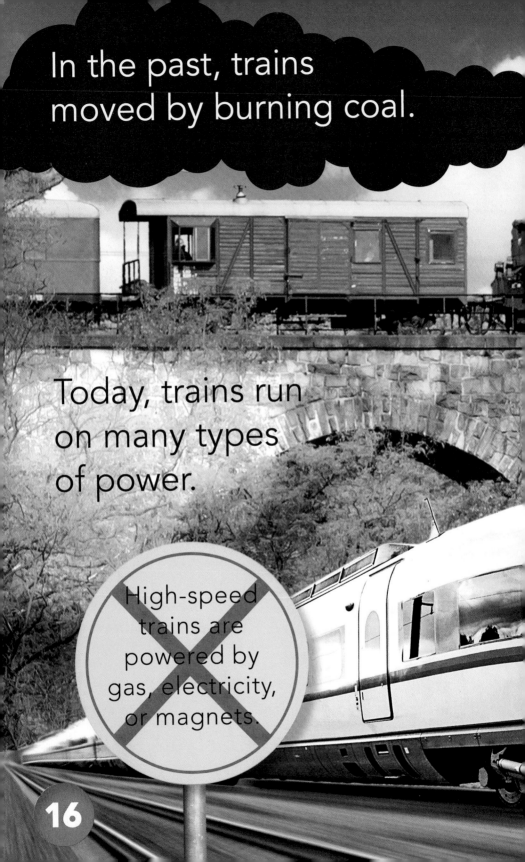

In the past, trains moved by burning coal.

Today, trains run on many types of power.

High-speed trains are powered by gas, electricity, or magnets.

16

Many people ride together on public transportation.

London
First (1863)

Beijing
*Longest
(274 miles)*

Boston
*First in the
US (1897)*

Tokyo
*Busiest (3.15 billion
rides per year)*

**New
York
City**
*Busiest in the US
(1.6 billion rides per year);
most stations (468)*

B444

School buses seat lots of kids. Subways carry millions of people under the street.

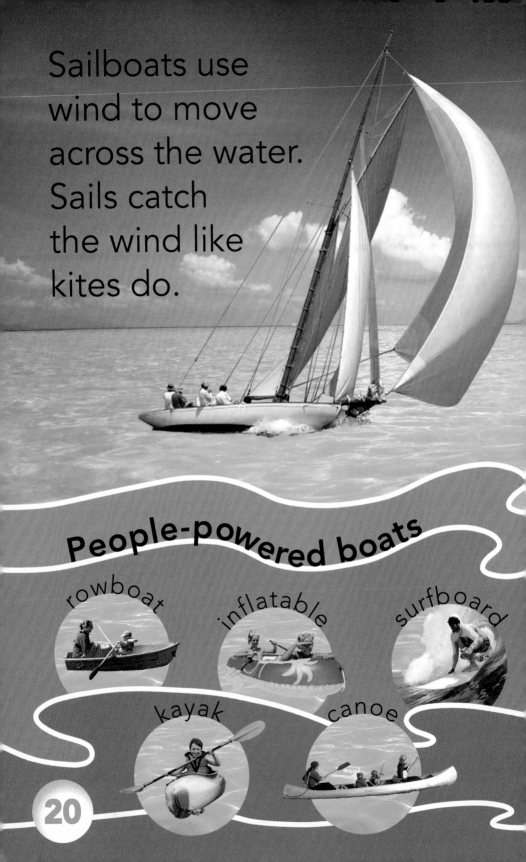

Sailboats use wind to move across the water. Sails catch the wind like kites do.

People-powered boats

rowboat

inflatable

surfboard

kayak

canoe

NEW WORD

surfing

SURF-ing

Ride the biggest waves when you go **surfing** at the beach.

SAY IT OUT LOUD

Motorboats use engines to move across the water.

Windsurfing is sailing plus surfing.

Big ships carry cargo over the ocean. They take weeks to travel far.

Container ship

Small tugboats help ships get to port. In port, cargo is taken off the ships.

NEW WORD
cargo
KAHR-goh
Anything that you buy in a store traveled there as **cargo.**
SAY IT OUT LOUD

Tugboat

23

Biplane

The first

At first, pilots flew alone in airplanes.

Today, most airplanes fit about 200 people.

Flying things

helicopter

seed

airplane flight was only 12 seconds long.

The biggest can hold more than 500.

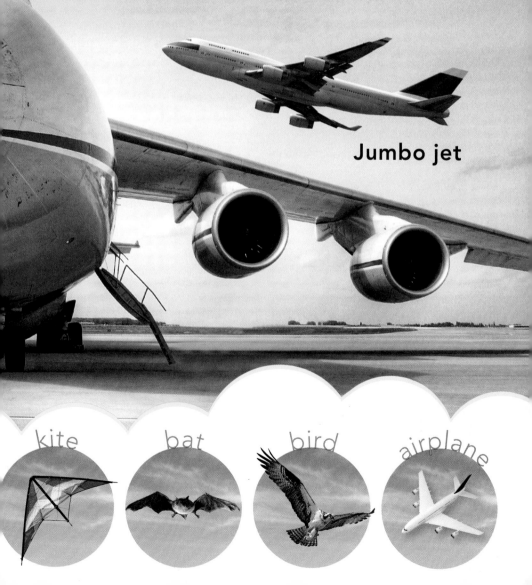

Jumbo jet

kite   bat   bird   airplane

Emergency! Call 911!
Help is on the way.

Fire truck

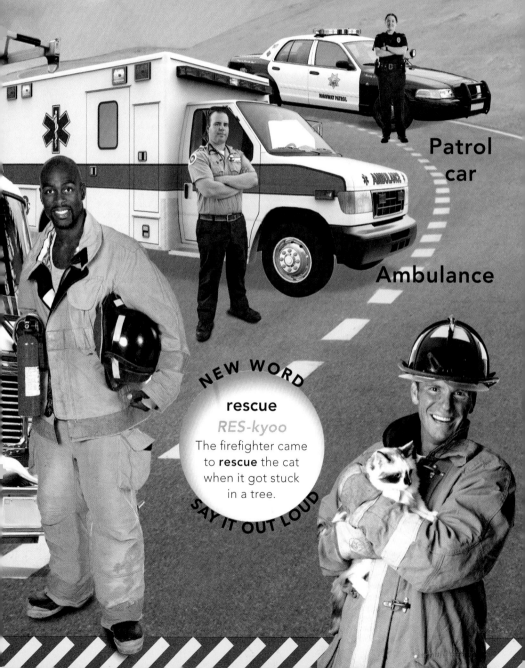

Rescue vehicles bring help to people who need it.

Helicopter

Patrol car

Ambulance

NEW WORD

rescue

RES-kyoo

The firefighter came to **rescue** the cat when it got stuck in a tree.

SAY IT OUT LOUD

Astronauts fly to space!
Rockets power their
spacecraft. They explore
beyond our planet.

NEIL ARMSTRONG

Neil Armstrong
was the first person
to walk on the Moon.
Before becoming an
astronaut, he worked
hard in school and in the
navy. He especially
loved science.

YOU CAN DO IT!

Rockets travel at more than 17,000 miles per hour.

Where will people go next? And how will they get there?

Glossary

ambulance
A truck with equipment to help people who are hurt.

astronaut
A person who flies into space.

biplane
An airplane with two sets of wings, one above and one below.

cargo
Goods that are carried by a ship or an aircraft.

championship
A contest that decides which team or player is the winner.

coal
A black rock burned as a fuel.

electricity
A kind of power that travels through wires.

emergency
A sudden danger to a person or people.

engine
A machine that makes something move.

gas
A fuel used in many kinds of transportation.

gear
A wheel that fits together with other wheels to change the movement in a machine.

goggles
Glasses that fit tightly around your eyes to protect them.

haul
To move a heavy load in a vehicle.

invent
To think up and make something new.

magnet
A piece of metal that pulls some other metals toward it.

motocross
A motorcycle race over rough ground.

port
A place where boats and ships can bring their cargo and stay safely.

power
The strength to move or do something.

rescue
To save someone who is in trouble.

subway
An electric train that runs underground in a city.

surfing
Standing on a surfboard and letting ocean waves carry you toward shore.

transportation
A system for moving people and things from one place to another.

Index

Image credits

Photography and artwork
1: Hupeng/Dreamstime; 2tl: Felifoto/Fotolia; 2bc: Spofi/Fotolia; 2–3b (grass): alinamd/Fotolia; 3 (balloons): Doug Sims/iStockphoto; 4 (girl x3): Paul Close/Scholastic Inc.; 4 (boy x3): Samuel Borges/Fotolia; 5 (sky): alinamd/Fotolia; 5 (airplane): Saorsa/Dreamstime; 5 (helicopter): Icholakov/Dreamstime; 5 (boat in water): Anatols/Dreamstime; 5 (motorcycle and rider): Janis Litavnieks/iStockphoto; 5 (truck): Drive Images/Alamy Images; 5 (woman in truck): Ruslan Dashinsky/iStockphoto; 5 (car): Motoring Picture Library/Alamy Images; 5 (man in car): Lorna/Dreamstime; 5 (bicycle and rider): Bowie15/Dreamstime; 6–7 (background): Paha_l/Dreamstime; 6tl: Hodag Media/Shutterstock; 6bl (wheel): Ivlius Costache/Dreamstime; 6bl (icon): filo/iStockphoto; 6–7 (main image): Lynne Sladky/AP Images; 7tr (boy on bicycle): iStockphoto/Thinkstock; 7tr (helmet): ipag/Dreamstime; 7br: Rob Fox/iStockphoto; 8–9 (background) iStockphoto/Thinkstock; 8–9 (main image): LOOK Die Bildagentur der Fotografen GmbH/Alamy Images; 8 (icon): Andrey Kokidko/Fotolia; 8bl: Dvmsimages/Dreamstime; 8bc: Bill Philpot/iStockphoto; 8br, 9bl: Stan Rohrer/iStockphoto; 9bc: 6thgearadvertising/Dreamstime; 9br: Shootalot/Dreamstime; 10–11 (sky): Matt_collingwood/Dreamstime; 10–11 (main image): Mark Evans/iStockphoto; 11 (icons): Cenker Atila/iStockphoto; 11tr: Action Sports Photography/Shutterstock; 11crt: Darren Brode/Shutterstock; 11crb: Lucie Lang/Shutterstock; 11br: Kosarev Alexander/Shutterstock; 12–13 (main image): Tips Images/SuperStock; 12tl: SSPL/Getty Images; 12tr: Library of Congress; 13tl: John Vachon/Library of Congress; 13tc: David Touchtone/Dreamstime; 13tr: Ltljtlj/Wikimedia; 13b: Kim Sohee/iStockphoto; 14–15 (background): alinamd/Fotolia; 14–15 (main image): Cdonofrio/Dreamstime; 15tr: Brian Myrick/AP Images; 15cr: Hakane/Dreamstime; 15br: Petrafler/Dreamstime; 16–17 (sky): Kk8737/Dreamstime; 16–17 (steam train, background): PHB.cz (Richard Semik)/Shutterstock; 16–17 (electric train): Ortodoxfoto/Dreamstime; 18t: Lya_Cattel/iStockphoto; 18 (bus icon): Kapreski/iStockphoto; 18–19b (subway): Panoramic Images/Getty Images; 18–19b (icons): angelha/Fotolia; 19t: kali9/iStockphoto; 20–21 (background): Martinma/Dreamstime; 20t: Giovanni Rinaldi/iStockphoto; 20 (rowboat): Britta Kasholm-Tengve/iStockphoto; 20 (inflatable): Maszas/Dreamstime; 20 (surfboard): Reniw-Imagery/iStockphoto; 20 (kayak): Olga Lyubkina/iStockphoto; 20 (canoe): Knud Nielsen/Dreamstime; 21t: Kirill Zdorov/Fotolia; 21bl: Forgiss/Dreamstime; 21br: Snaprender/iStockphoto; 22–23 (sky): Arkadi Bojarsinov/Dreamstime; 22–23 (container ship, water): Hans-Peter Merten/Getty Images; 23 (tugboat): jurand/Fotolia; 24–25 (main image): ncn18/Shutterstock; 24tl: Pascal Martin/Fotolia; 24bl: hypergon/iStockphoto; 24b (sky background): Matt_collingwood/Dreamstime; 24bc: iStockphoto/Thinkstock; 24br: joanna wnuk/Fotolia; 25t (banner): Biggie Productions/Getty Images; 25cr: blackred/iStockphoto; 25bl: iStockphoto/Thinkstock; 25bcl: nn-fotografie/Fotolia; 25bcr: Brian Kushner/Dreamstime; 26tl: Leontura/iStockphoto; 26–27 (sky): Kk8737/Dreamstime; 26–27 (road, grass): Okea/Dreamstime; 26b: Terri Francis/Shutterstock; 27tr: Daniel Cardiff/iStockphoto; 27 (firefighter bl): sjlocke/iStockphoto; 27 (ambulance): nerthuz/Fotolia; 27 (paramedic): Heather Nemec/iStockphoto; 27 (patrol car): Patronu/Dreamstime; 27 (police officer): Iofoto/Dreamstime; 27br: jonya/iStockphoto; 28–29 (background t): Igorkovalchuk/Dreamstime; 28–29 (background b): clearviewstock/Fotolia; 28cr: NASA; 28b: Science Source; 29tl: Jacques70/Dreamstime; 29tr: Orla/Dreamstime; 29 (icon): Sam/Fotolia; 29c: Jack Frassanito and Associates/NASA; 30–31: Fuse/Thinkstock; 32 (stars background): Igorkovalchuk/Dreamstime; 32 (rocket): Sam/Fotolia; 32 (Moon): Nerss/Dreamstime; 32 (clouds background): Kk8737/Dreamstime; 32 (boats): Patrick Ellis/iStockphoto; 32 (airplane): Vladimiraz/Dreamstime; 32 (bicycle l): filo/iStockphoto; 32 (motorcycle): Petrafler/Dreamstime; 32 (race car): Julydfg/Dreamstime; 32 (truck): Kim Sohee/iStockphoto; 32 (bicycle r): Hakane/Dreamstime; 32 (fire truck): Leontura/iStockphoto.

Cover
Front cover: (train icon) Neal Cobourne/Scholastic Inc.; (airplane icon) Oculo/Dreamstime; (car icon, motorcycle icon) Julydfg/Dreamstime; (boat icon) Neal Cobourne/Scholastic Inc.; (b) David Madison/Corbis Images. Back cover: (computer monitor) Manaemedia/Dreamstime. Inside front cover: (t) Oktay Degirmenci/iStockphoto; (c) Scholastic Inc.; (b) Cenker Atila/iStockphoto.